W9-BTL-333

9/06

Shorewood – Troy Library
650 Deerwood Drive
Shorewood, IL 60404
815-725-1715

1.6

A Tadpole Grows Up

by
Pam Zollman

Children's Press®
A Division of Scholastic Inc.
New York Toronto London Auckland Sydney
Mexico City New Delhi Hong Kong
Danbury, Connecticut

SHOREWOOD-TROY LIBRARY
650 DEERWOOD DRIVE
SHOREWOOD, IL 60431

These content vocabulary word builders
are for grades 1-2.

Consultant: Roy McDiarmid
Research Zoologist and Curator of Amphibians
National Museum of Natural History
Smithsonian Institution, Washington, D.C.

Curriculum Specialist: Linda Bullock

Special thanks to the Kansas City Zoo

Photo Credits:
Photographs © 2005: Dan Suzio Photography: back cover, cover left inset, 1, 2, 4 bottom, 5 top right, 5 bottom left, 6, 7, 8, 10, 11, 12, 13, 17, 20, 21; Dembinsky Photo Assoc.: 4 top, 14 (DPA), 19 top (Skip Moody); Dwight R. Kuhn Photography: cover background, 5 top left, 5 bottom right, 9, 15,19 bottom, 23 top right, 23 bottom left; Michael Durham/www.Durmphoto.com: 23 top left; Photo Researchers, NY: cover right inset (David N. Davis), cover center inset (Gary Meszaros); Tom & Pat Leeson: 23 bottom right.

Book Design: Simonsays Design!

Library of Congress Cataloging-in-Publication Data

Zollman, Pam.
A tadpole grows up / by Pam Zollman. p. cm.–(Scholastic news nonfiction readers)
Includes bibliographical references and index.
ISBN 0-516-24947-9 (lib. bdg.) 0-516-24797-2 (pbk.)
1. Tadpoles–Development–Juvenile literature. I. Title. II. Series.
QL668.E2Z65 2005
597.8'139–dc22

2005002086

Copyright © 2005 by Scholastic Inc.
All rights reserved. Published simultaneously in Canada.
Printed in the United States of America
CHILDREN'S PRESS and associated logos are trademarks and or registered trademarks of Scholastic Library Publishing. SCHOLASTIC and associated logos are trademarks and or registered trademarks of Scholastic Inc.

1 2 3 4 5 6 7 8 9 10 R 14 13 12 11 10 09 08 07 06 05

CONTENTS

WORD HUNT

Look for these words as you read. They will be in **bold**.

algae
(**al**-jee)

embryo
(**em**-bree-oh)

string
(string)

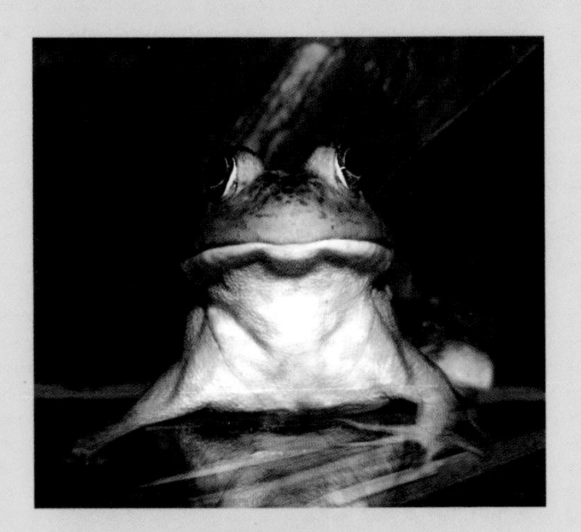

amphibian
(am-**fib**-ee-uhn)

blob
(blahb)

tadpole
(**tad**-pole)

worm
(wurm)

Tadpoles!

Are those fish?

No, they are **tadpoles**.

Tadpoles grow into frogs or toads.

These tadpoles will grow into toads.

Frogs and toads
are **amphibians**.

Amphibians live in water
and on land.

Frogs have smooth skin.

Toads have bumpy skin.

Look at the smooth skin on this frog.

Toads and frogs lay eggs in lakes, ponds, and puddles.

Frogs lay eggs in a **blob**.

Toads lay eggs in a **string**.

Jelly covers the eggs to keep them safe.

frog egg blob

Toad eggs look like strings.

Embryos grow inside the eggs.

The eggs will hatch in about 2 to 3 weeks.

The embryos become tadpoles when they hatch.

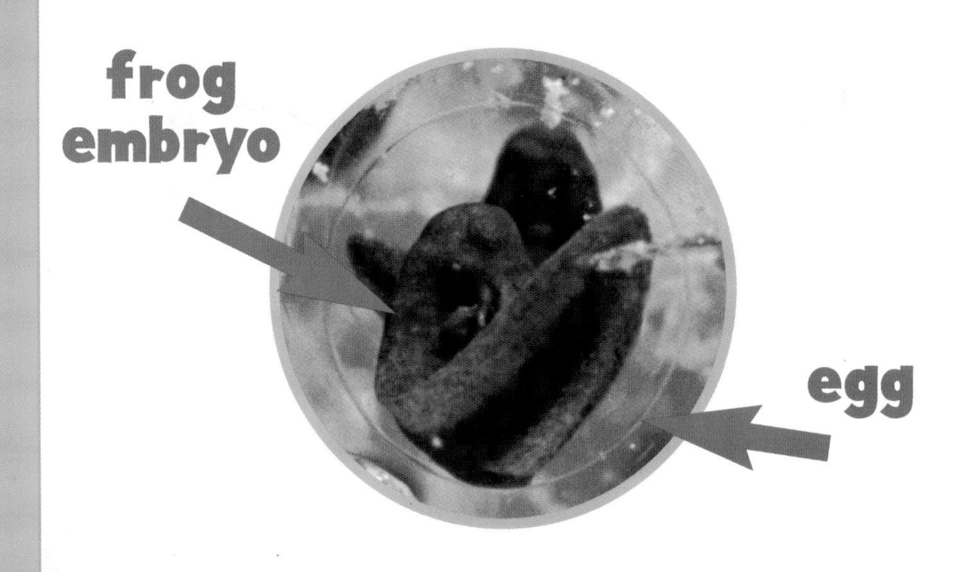

Look! These frog eggs will hatch soon.

A tadpole looks like a fish.

It has a tail, but no legs.

Its gills help it get air from the water.

It eats **algae**. Algae are plants that live in water.

This frog tadpole is swimming in algae.

What is happening to
this tadpole?

It is growing back legs.

Its front legs will
grow later.

Its lungs are growing, too.

Its lungs help it to
breathe air.

legs

Three months have passed.

The tadpole has lost its tail.

It's time to hop out
of the water!

The tadpole eats bugs
and **worms** now.

Tadpoles can grow into toads.

Tadpoles can grow into frogs.

A Tadpole Grows Up!

1

Jelly covers the eggs to keep the frog eggs safe. Embryos are inside the eggs.

2

Look! This egg is about to hatch. When the egg hatches, a tadpole comes out.

3

These tadpoles are 10 days old.

7

Where's the tail? It's gone! The tadpole is grown up. It is a frog now.

6

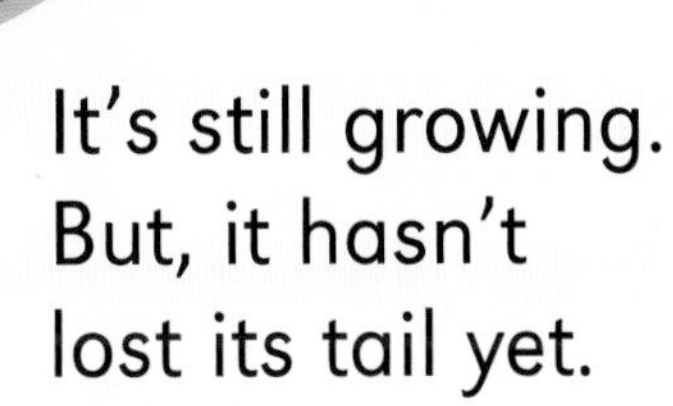

It's still growing. But, it hasn't lost its tail yet.

5

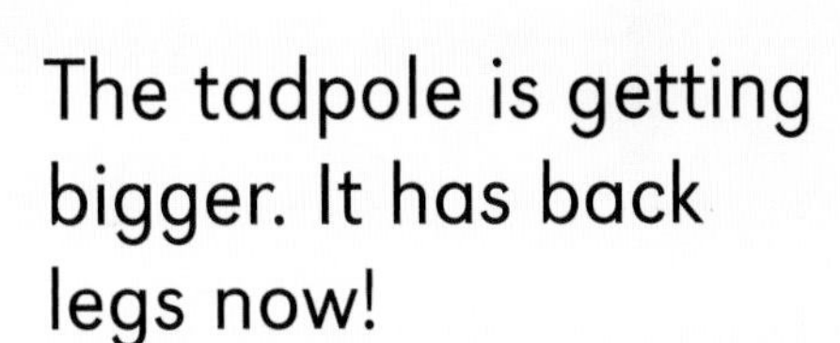

The tadpole is getting bigger. It has back legs now!

4

This tadpole is hungry. Look at it eat!

SHOREWOOD-TROY LIBRARY
650 DEERWOOD DRIVE
SHOREWOOD, IL 60431

YOUR NEW WORDS

algae (**al**-jee) very tiny plants that grow in water that do not have roots or stems

amphibian (am-**fib**-ee-uhn) an animal that hatches in water

blob (blahb) a frog lays a group, or blob of eggs

embryo (**em**-bree-oh) a baby animal that grows inside an egg

string (string) a toad lays a string of eggs

tadpole (**tad**-pole) a young frog or toad that lives in water, breathes through gills, and has a tail, but no legs

worm (wurm) a small animal that lives in the soil

THESE ANIMALS LAY EGGS IN THE WATER, TOO!

jellyfish

newt

salamander

trout

INDEX

FIND OUT MORE

Book:

Face to Face: Frogs, Scholastic Inc., 2001

Website:

http://www.enchantedlearning.com/subjects/amphibians/Frog/

MEET THE AUTHOR:

Pam Zollman is the award-winning author of short stories, articles, and books for kids. She is the author of other Life Cycles books in the Scholastic News Nonfiction Readers series. She lives in rural Pennsylvania and has played with tadpoles, toads, and frogs. Tree frogs are her favorite.